OLDER GUY

Poems

By Tom Carnicelli

TABLE OF CONTENTS

A Note to the Reader

In the epilogue to my first collection, *Old Guy, Part One*, I promised not to write an *Old Guy, Part Two*. I haven't really kept that promise. I found that I did have more to say about getting used to old age and retirement.

I also promised not to write about depressing things like sickness and death. That promise I've kept pretty well, breaking it only once (or twice). I'm afraid, though, that this collection is not quite as amusing as the first one. I'm not sure why. Maybe I'm a bit more mellow.

I've expanded my scope a bit. Most of the poems are still about people, but I've added a few about old places and things. And I've added a few about my favorite season, winter, which seems by far the oldest of the seasons, at least here in New England.

York, Maine
October 2017

1

GROWING OLDER

Turning Eighty

"I can't believe it," she said,
"You can't possibly be eighty."
She seemed truly shocked.
Most people seem surprised
(Or so they say) when they find out
How old I am, and I take
Their reactions as compliments.

It's great when people tell you
You don't look your age.
The only problem is that you are
Your age.

PLAYING THE PART

I played the part of old man again today.
I'm getting pretty good at it.

My forgetfulness is much improved.
My wife will tell me something and,
An hour later, I'll act as if I'd never
Heard of it before.

My old man's crabbiness is quite
Convincing, especially when my wife
Asks me to put down the newspaper
And help her with something.

My body itself has become part
Of the act. I use my aching back
And tired feet to walk like an old man,
Bending over a little and dragging
My feet in a kind of shuffle.
And, when I play an old man
Sleeping, I can actually fall asleep
In my chair.

They say a role can take over
An actor. I'd better watch out.

Paterfamilias

The familiar table is all set,
With bouquets of small pink roses
At intervals along the center.
At each place, a yellow napkin
Is tucked in a napkin ring
Shaped like an Easter bunny.

We file in and take our seats.
The seat at the head of the table
Is still empty, the seat for the head
Of the family, the paterfamilias.
I can remember my grandfather
Sitting in that chair, and,
After him, my own father. Neither
Of them is going to show up
To take it today. It's my seat now.

I suppose I look the part -
I'm an old guy with white hair -,
But I don't feel comfortable sitting here.
I'm used to seeing my elders in this role,
And I don't feel like an elder just yet.

LOSING IT

I drove half way from Boston
With my signal light on.
That disturbed me. It led me to ask
The big question we old guys ask:
"Am I losing it?"

I do plenty of dumb things:
Forget to return calls,
Wear ill-matched clothes,
Fall asleep at the dinner table;
I'm always late.

I've been doing these things
For years. They make me
Hard to live with, but they're nothing new,
Nothing like driving forty miles
With the blinker on.

I don't think I'm losing it
Just yet, but I do have to question.
And there's one thing I do know for sure:
The day I stop asking the question,
The answer will be "Yes."

Contemporaries

The deceased was five years
Older than me, and his time
Had clearly come. It wasn't his death
That bothered me; it was how
The mourners looked. Their clothes
Were fine- dark suits, tasteful dresses -
But it was a shock to see how people
I hadn't seen for a while had aged.
These were people whose faces I'd seen
Almost every day; now, I could barely
Recognize them. And there was an old guy
Moving very unsteadily down the aisle
Who used to beat me in tennis.
(Could he possibly beat me now?)

When I look at my own face
In the mirror, I can't see much change.
Contemporaries are the mirror
That shows the truth.

Body Changes

SELF-IMPROVEMENT

I went to my dentist today
And ordered two new front teeth.
My old ones are chipped, uneven,
And not exactly pearly white.
When my teeth look better,
I know I'll smile more often.

And I've just had laser surgery
On my eyes. Now, I can see
The road signs from a distance -
No swerving or missing the turn.
And no more waving at strangers
Or failing to recognize friends.

My ears are my next project.
I hate sitting at the dinner table
With a painted smile. I hate saying
"I didn't catch that," and my wife
Must be tired of hearing it
(She needs to speak up, though).

Down the road, there are bigger
Things to consider - new knees,
New hips. No need for them yet,
But my friends have had them
And their lives have improved. Even
Their golf scores have improved.

At this point, it's foolish to spend
Money on externals. Spend it
Instead on improving yourself,
Part by part by part.

WALKING TALL

"Don't walk like an old man,"
My wife says. I know I'm not doing
The legs-apart, load-in-the-pants walk.
I do that only after riding my bike or sitting
Too long in the car, times when my legs
Barely move at all. I must be doing
The other old man's walk, the one
Where you bend forward at the waist,
Pull your head forward and down,
And walk on your toes like a chicken.
I do that one a lot.

It's easy enough to correct.
Head up! Shoulders back! Eyes front!
There, I feel younger already.

Sleeping

When I was working, I'd try
To get eight hours of sleep a night.
I still do. But the hours are different.
Then, it was eleven to seven.
Now, it's usually eight to four.

If you're an old guy like me,
It's hard to stay awake after you eat
Your evening meal. If I sit down
In a comfortable chair after dinner,
I'm out like a light, and snoring loudly
(So I'm told). After an hour or two,
My wife will call from our bedroom
And wake me up. And then I'll stagger
Up the stairs and flop into bed,
Asleep again instantly.

But only until four. I wake up at four
Every morning. It's too early to get up,
But lying there in bed from four to six
Is not a happy time. The world looks
Bleak, full and full of problems.
I lie there, worrying, and, if I doze off,
Nightmares wake me. I'm relieved
When daylight finally comes.

I might be able to sleep through
To six if I could stay up later,
Maybe until ten or so. But that's
Much easier said than done.
We old guys tend not to stay up late.
We conk out early.

THE RIGHT FIT

When you get older, your body
Changes, but your clothes don't.
Your pants, especially, become a problem.
A bulging waistline you can work on,
But there's another, more subtle change
That diet or exercise can't touch.

All my pants are too long now.
They bunch up at my ankles,
And I keep stepping on the cuffs.
On some of them, the fabric is starting
To fray quite badly. "They look,"
My wife says, "like thrift-shop rejects,"
But she's willing to mend them.

Mother Nature is also willing to help.
Two years ago, I shrank my favorite
Black pants. They came up too high
On my ankles, and I couldn't wear them.
Last year, they fit a little better.
Next year, they'll probably fit just fine.

BIKING UPHILL

Today, we biked through a series
Of long and steep hills. I couldn't do it.
I got off and walked every time.
Maybe I've gotten too old for biking up
Big hills. Perhaps If I were younger
(Much younger), I might have done it.

Probably not. These hills are tough.
You look up and all you see is more road
Leading upward to more road. I doubt
I could have scaled them at twenty.
I might have climbed a little higher,
But I suspect I would have pooped out
Before getting to the top.

Sure, I'm not as strong as I was,
But I was never Charles Atlas to begin with.
And I'm not the Ninety-Eight Pound Weakling
Right now; I'm a strong biker in good shape.
These hills are too damn long and steep.
Peeling sixty years off this body
Wouldn't help me scale them.

CARRYING ON

I Don't Miss It

Deciding to retire is final,
Just like deciding to divorce.
Friends I know who've decided
To divorce will not be persuaded
To reconsider, despite the pleas
Of their shocked friends.
They've made up their minds,
Once and for all.

And so it was for me,
But with one big difference.
My job was not at all
Like a troubled marriage.
It was a wonderful job.
I enjoyed it right to the end.
But I can't say I miss it now.
The end was the end.

FEELING O.K.

Once a year, I see my finance guy.
He explains my situation, in detail.
I forget it all, of course, as soon
As I leave his office. Still, I leave
Feeling confident: he didn't seem
Concerned. My financial future
Seems to be O.K.

I see my doctor twice a year.
He tells me I should exercise more,
That my bad cholesterol is higher
Than it should be, things I remember
Because I hear them every year.
I promise to do better, and leave
Feeling relieved: he wasn't that
Concerned. For now, my health
Is O.K., too.

Most old guys don't have
Long-range plans. I certainly don't.
I don't have a bucket list,
And I don't want a second career
(Even if the Red Sox or the Patriots
Should call me). If I can stay
Healthy and solvent a while longer,
I'm O.K. with that.

At the Gym

When it finally played,
We all knew we'd found our theme song.
Our gym radio plays Golden Oldies
Non-stop, music from the eras we all
Grew up in: Petula Clark, Roy Orbison,
Diana Ross and the Supremes.
Our average age is probably
In the mid-seventies, and, for once,
I'm not the oldest in the group.
There's a couple here, both 89,
Who push the average up.
We're all pretty dedicated. We're here
Every morning at six a.m.,
Hot summer and frigid winter.
(This is Northern New England.)
Most of us stay at least an hour.
We work on weight machines,
On rowing machines, on tread mills.
We all know each other, and there's
A lot of banter. We chew over
The local news and politics.
We talk about sports and movies
And books. We talk (not that often)
About our ailments. Some of us
Are recovering from surgeries;
Two guys have to use oxygen tanks;
Most of us, like my wife and me,
Are just trying to stay healthy.
We're all after the same thing, and,
When the Beegees sing "Staying Alive,"
We know they're singing for us.

Late in the Season

We're cycling along the Elbe river
In a steady drizzle, a troop of retirees
On a week-long biking trip. It's a Friday
In October, and we've had rain
For five days straight.

We don't let it bother us. We've
Been through worse things than a stretch
Of bad weather. We put on our gaudy gear -
Red or yellow or neon green -
And stay on our route.

The river cafes are trying to hold
On to summer. Their tables are still out.
Those under cover have napkins and silver.
The ones in the open are glazed
With rainwater.

How pleasant it would be
To sit in one of these charming places
On a bright summer day, with a perfect view
Of the river and the little towns
On the other shore.

Maybe next year. Right now,
All we want is to keep on riding,
To ride harder as the rain gets stronger,
To push right on into the heart
Of the old city.

There, we'll stash our bikes,
Check into our hotel, change
Out of these wet biking clothes, shower;
Then meet in the hotel bar at six,
Our usual time.

Advice

NOT ENTITLED

You're comfortable. You think
Nothing you do now matters,
That you yourself are nothing but
A harmless old man.

Not so. Nobody's harmless.
As long as you're still living,
You still have plenty of chances
To do people harm.

You can still be a bore
Or a complainer or a tyrant.
You can still hurt your friends,
Or make your wife unhappy.

You're not entitled
To be a selfish incompetent
Just because you're old. You're still
In the game. Play your part.

THE STARVING ARMENIANS

During World War Two,
When my father was away
In the Navy, my mother kept
The papers out of my sight.

I read them now, every day,
And I can see why she hid them.
Today's wars aren't as big, but
The pictures are just as painful.

It's the pictures of the survivors
That stick in my mind, people
Who have lost everything -
Loved ones, homes, possessions.

I'd like to help them, but how?
I'm sitting here, enjoying
My usual breakfast, and they're
In Syria, starving to death.

Maybe I can use my mother's
Logic (it's every mother's logic).
"Clean your plate," She'd say,
"Think of the starving Armenians."

And so I cleaned my plate,
But I couldn't see how it would do
The starving Armenians much good.
And I'll clean it again today.

BUYING WINE

We go to a wine shop and the woman there
Tells us about each wine. She explains how
The type of grape, the climate, and the region
All affect the taste; how, in the same region,
Wines made from the same type of grape
Will vary with the amount of sun and rain
Each vineyard gets.

We're impressed by her knowledge,
And happy enough to take her suggestions,
But I feel like a swine when we leave.
My old wine-buying habits will not improve.
I buy by color, by type, and by price.
I can also be influenced by the design
Of the label.

CATCHING UP

Now that I'm retired,
I can focus on problems
I've neglected all my life:
My posture, for instance.

My father always told me
To pull my shoulders back
And stand up straight.
I haven't done that well.

With more time available,
I can focus on this problem,
And on others things
Grown-up people should do:

Like eating a good breakfast,
Brushing after every meal,
Wearing clean underwear,
Keeping my room clean.

I hope to work very hard now
To master these basic tasks.
I might even tackle some new ones,
Like learning to be patient.

THE SPECIALS

Being retired is a blast,
Especially in winter, when
All the restaurants have specials.
Every restaurant has a special day.
Just mark them on your calendar.
You can eat out on specials
Every night of the week.

Start with Happy Hour.
All the bars have free hors-doeuvres
And five-dollar cocktails.
Then, move on to the restaurant
With the special for the night.
They have some fantastic deals:
Dollar oysters, five-dollar burgers,
All the spaghetti you can eat,
And the two you just can't beat -
Twin lobsters for twenty bucks,
Two entrees for the price of one.

Perhaps you and your lovely wife
Would like to join us some evening.
We'll be dining with some other retired guys
(And their lovely wives). Just find
The restaurant with the evening special
And ask for us by name.
All the waiters know us.

PARENTS

OLD PARENTS

We all worry about our Old Parents.
"Dad really shouldn't be driving,
But how else can they get by?"
"Mom's losing it, but Dad's too frail
To take proper care of her."
" We can't hire help for them - they won't
Let strangers into the house."
The same worries, the same problems.
We try to help them and they
Try never to be a burden.

For the past twenty years,
I've been a child every day and a parent
On permanent stand-by. Now,
I'm just a parent, and an old one at that.
How soon before I become a burden, a source
Of worry and concern for my own children?
Maybe I already am, but I don't think so.
At least I hope not. I'm hoping
There'll still be a good long while
Before the worm finally turns.

PHONE CALLS

My mother didn't get out much.
Mostly, she sat in her white leather chair
By the window. She had a fine view
Of the harbor, but, one day,
She told me she couldn't see it -
Not the boats, not the water -
It was all "a blank white blur."
She couldn't see the big T.V. either.
When the evening news was on,
She was really just listening.
She had to give up reading, too.
Even the Large Print books
Couldn't help. But she still could hear.
She listened to novels on audio books,
Even Gone With the Wind.

She insisted that my wife and I keep
Taking trips, and she loved to hear
About them. I liked to call her
From unusual places, and, one time,
I called her around ten at night.
(I knew she'd be up, listening to some book.)
"Guess where we are, Mom."
"We're on a boat in New York harbor,
Out by the Statue of Liberty."
I did my best to describe it all: how few
Lights there were around the Statue,
How close to it we were, how huge
It looked looming over us,
How excited the people got,
How many languages they spoke.
The call took twenty minutes.

My mother always remembered
That scene, and so do I.
I wonder if I'd remember it so well
If I hadn't described it to her.

BUON FIGLIO

for Stanley

It was a blessing.
Everyone knows that.
Still, she was your mother,
And, in those long days sitting
By her bed, you kept looking
For a sign of her old self.
And if, by some miracle,
That old self had returned,
You were ready to whisk her off
For drinks and dinner at the Wentworth
Or, better yet, the Four Seasons.

It didn't happen, of course, and yet
It did happen before. You did take her
To such places, often, and you two
Had many good times together.
Remember those times now -
How she looked, what she said.
That was who your mother was,
And you were there beside her,
A good and faithful son.

My Father's Letters

Not everybody gets to be
Fifty years older than his own father,
But that's my situation now.
I'm reading letters my father wrote
To my mother when he was still
In college. This was not the serious,
Disciplined adult I knew.
He was a serious student, sure,
But he was playful, even silly at times.
He liked puns and ridiculous jokes.
He wrote long, philosophical stories
And an occasional poem. His letters
Were (are) great fun to read.
My mother must have enjoyed them.
She kept them all in a hatbox
I found in her bedroom closet.

I wish I had her letters to him.
All I know is that he sometimes
Had a few too many drinks
On their Saturday nights.
Several of his letters are full
Of apologies and promises.
She must have given him hell.
(And he probably deserved it.)

But, come on, Ma.
This is the guy who'll support
Us all, the guy the whole family
Will rely on. Give him a break.
And, of course, she did.

Parents and Children

"The Baby's Coming"

"The baby's coming! The baby's coming!"
"When, next week?" "No, next July."
That's four months away, but already
The laundry room has become "the baby's room."
And soon, baby items begin to appear:
Cute little outfits, plastic toys that make noises
(One even plays Beethoven's "Ode to Joy").
Every week brings some new little item.
We lack the big items, though - not surprising
Since we haven 't had a baby stay in this house
For around fifty years. We had an old crib
In our attic for a while but gave it away.
Our friends, of course, have nothing either.
Still, there's a network in these matters, and,
By mid-June, there's a crib, a changing station,
And a high chair ready in our attic.

The baby arrived in July, as scheduled.
She slept in her crib in her room and she ate
In her high chair and she wore the cute outfits
And she played with the plastic toys
And she played and she laughed (and she cried)
And everyone loved to see and hear her.
And then she left and went back home.

It's the laundry room again and there's
A pile of old guy's socks and underwear
Where the changing station used to stand.
The house is quiet again, and, after all that
Preparation, was that little one-week visit
Really worth it? Yes, it was.

Adult Conversation

This is ridiculous. Here we are,
A bunch of intelligent adults,
And we're not talking to one another.
All our attention is focused on this baby,
This two-year-old who can barely talk at all.
It's cocktail time, and she learns to say "carrot"
And "cracker" and "peanut."
She holds up each item and sings out its name,
As if to say "Look at this wonderful thing."
It is fun to watch her, but enough's enough,
And her parents take her off to bed.

Now the adult conversation can begin.
We start with presidential politics, but
Get nowhere fast. Most of us hate
Both candidates. We shift to the old favorite,
Other people's ailments. Mary's operation
Went well, but she'll have to do chemo.
Bill Murphy looks like hell - he's lost at least
Thirty pounds - does he have cancer?
Betty Eames is walking with a cane now-
She'll get a hip replacement this fall.
Joe has Lyme disease. Louise has shingles.
Harry's hemorrhoids ... And so it goes.

Somebody go wake up the baby.

WONDER WOMAN

When I was born,
My mother was kept in the hospital
For two full weeks. She was perfectly healthy,
But that's how things were done
Way back in the day.

Young mothers today
Don't want or need pampering.
They sprint by our houses, pushing their babies
In carriages; one even sprints with
A double carriage.

They do amazing feats,
But the mother I saw this morning
Topped them all. She had a baby strapped
To her chest and a big white dog
Tugging at her hand.

When the dog stopped
And relieved himself on my front lawn,
I expected the woman to walk right on,
And I wouldn't have blamed her.
What else could she do?

The baby began
Waving its arms and crying,
And the dog began tugging again in earnest,
But she stayed right there. She bent over,
Reached her free hand down,

Scooped the pile
Into her little green bag, slipped
The bag into her pocket, and went on her way,
Leaving me to wonder: Who was that woman?
Where were her mask and cape?

BIG GUYS

Males can be huge. That man
Sitting by the window is one big guy.
He's wearing shorts and a t-shirt,
And his arms and legs and stomach
Seem stuffed into his clothes, with no slack,
No room to spare. Even his fingers
Seem full to the bursting point.
Across the table is a jolly little fellow,
No doubt his son. The father must weigh
At least 250; the son, around 20.
It's hard to believe that such a huge man
Was once so small; but he was.
And it's hard to believe that the little guy
Could ever become so big;
But I'll bet he will.

HUSBAND AND WIFE

THE ACID TEST

This is it, the acid test.
We're both retired now
And living at home, together
All day long.

We haven't killed
Each other yet. We snap
And bicker over trivial things,
But on things that really matter
We work it out.

We spend time with friends,
But usually it's just the two of us,
From six a.m., when we're at the gym,
To eleven at night, when we're lying in bed,
Watching the news.

We get along fine,
Except when she says she "can't
Live in this messy house another minute."
Then, I know that the spirit of extreme cleanliness
Has come upon her.

I rise from my chair,
Pick up the newspaper, and go and sit
In the bathroom.

SEATBELTING

When I turn on the car, my wife
Says "Seatbelt." I don't respond.
As I head down the driveway,
She'll say "Please put on
Your seat belt." I don't respond,
And pull out onto the road.
At her third (or fourth) request,
I will reach back for the damn thing
And jam it in place, while the car
Lurches from side to side.
"That's so dangerous," my wife says.
"it's also stupid.," she adds.
I have to admit (to myself)
She's right. It is dangerous.
And stupid, too.

Today, my wife was away,
And I had errands to do.
I put on my seat belt, even
Before I started the car,
Every single time.

Because I missed her.

Marital Problems

I can make fun of it,
But my wife's anxiety
When I'm driving is genuine;
She really is scared.

I try not to let it
Upset me, and, at times,
I know she's saved us both
From harm.

Still, it's unnerving
To have her suck in
Her breath or cry "Watch out"
For no good reason.

I start to question
Myself. Like any old guy,
I'm always worried about
Losing some ability.

And If I lose
Confidence in my ability
To drive, then we really are
In danger.

I do offer
To let her drive, but she
Usually declines. (When she drives,
I just fall asleep.)

It's one more
Problem that we probably
Won't solve, like my nightly snoring
In our marital bed.

DINING ALONE

My wife and I were having lunch
When a man came in, hung up his hat
And coat, and took a seat at the bar.
He was a well-dressed older man,
Wearing a tweed jacket and a dress shirt,
Open at the collar. He was well-groomed,
With none of those little grooming problems
That men who have lost their wives often have -
No stray hairs on his collar or shoulders,
No spots on his neat, uncrumpled jacket.
He was clearly a regular here. The barkeeper
Addressed him by name and brought
His cocktail unasked for.

I don't know, of course, that he was
A widower. Maybe his wife was lunching
With friends. Maybe she was at Yoga class.
Maybe he'd never had a wife at all,
Maybe I was just imagining how I might live
If my own wife should die before me.
She, too, thought he had the look
Of a man who had lost a wife -
A good one, she added.

She and I

She always has plans;
I never do. This morning,
She'll go to the gym; then,
Drop off our winter clothes
At the dry-cleaners; then,
Pick up some food for supper.
She'll be home around noon.
While she's gone, I'll be drinking
Coffee and reading the paper,
Indefinitely. If all goes well,
I should be dressed and shaved
By the time she gets back.

Why are women so good
At retirement, and men so bad?
My wife left the house at 7
Every morning for forty years.
When she retired, she never
Looked back, never sat around
Feeling morose; she found
Things to do, and did them.
When I retired (after fifty years),
I accomplished nothing for at least
A full year, and, even now,
I'm often at loose ends.

Why the difference? I know
All the theories about gender roles,
But maybe the answer is more simple.
Maybe women are just better at living.

OLD POSSESSIONS

Save It for Later

It's later now.
You saved all this stuff for later,
And now it still sits here,
Fifty years later, a tall pile
Of used lumber: two-by-fours
With nails sticking out of them;
Moldings of various sizes
And lengths;
Floor boards, some soft
And unfinished, some rock-hard
And lacquered.
This wood is strong and dry
Beneath its coating of dust.
It could still be used.

But who's going to use it?
You didn't. You've kept it here
All these years and barely touched it.
You couldn't bear to throw
It out. It was good, solid wood;
It had value. And so it did,
And so it would still -
To the right person in the right
Circumstance.
But the right person will never
Come to this cellar to find it.
If you leave it here now,
Your son will be stuck with it,
And he'll be tempted
To keep it around longer.
Do him a favor: call somebody;
Have it hauled away.

DISPOSING OF THINGS

Your children get first choice.
Anything they want, they can have.
But they won't want much, and you can
Quickly move on to Plan B:
If it has practical value, sell it,
Or give it away to some charity;
If it has no practical value, then just
Throw it in the trash.

I've tried to follow Plan B,
But there are limits. Certain items
With no practical value whatsoever
I just can't throw away:
The books I've collected,
Old and highly specialized;
All the notes and hand-outs I created
To teach my own courses.

Nobody but me would ever
Want to use these things, and,
Quite frankly, I myself will never touch
Most of them again.
Still, I want to keep them.
I'm proud of them. That library
Took years to build. Those course materials
Are some of my finest work.

I want them to sit there
In my study until I go. And then,
My heirs have my cheerful permission
To throw them in the trash.

Mundane Tasks

I was cleaning out my files
The other day. What a pile of stuff!
I kept most of the personal things:
Pictures of celebrations;
Letters from family and friends; even
Some very sentimental poems
From my youthful, Romantic period.
Most of the papers from my work
I threw away.

All those careful reports
And proposals I wrote for my work
No longer mattered to anyone.
I saved a few papers that involve
Issues that are still current.
I might read those again some day.
The rest of the materials, probably
Ninety percent of the stuff,
I just threw in the trash.

But not because I think
That work was a waste of my time.
I don't regret the efforts I made.
Mundane tasks matter.
We all have to do the dishes
And mop the floors, but we don't
Need to read about it later.

GREEN ROCKERS

You've probably seen
One of those old seaside hotels,
With a long, wide front porch
And a long row of green rocking chairs.
Well, we bought six of those chairs
When the Ocean House went under,
And we use them every summer,
On our own front porch.

Our house isn't a hotel, but it feels
Like one when all the relatives
And friends arrive. (Not that we mind.)
I put the rockers out by Memorial Day.
In July and August, they get plenty
Of use: there are always people in them,
Reading or chatting, and, at five o'clock,
We're all out there for cocktails.

Our guests leave by September,
But I still keep the rockers out. They don't
Get much use. Maybe I'll sit in one
As I read the paper. Maybe a neighbor
Will drop over for a drink. Mostly,
The rockers just sit there empty.
After Thanksgiving, I'll take them in,
Before the snow comes.

OLD PLACES AND SCENES

First of December

Autumn's work is done.
The trees are finally stripped
Of their leaves. The grass is brown.
The snow could arrive any day now
(And that's fine with me), but,
Before then, take a look around.
For this is it, what the earth really is,
Without leaves or snow to disguise it.
It's a world of trees - elms, maples, oaks -
Each with its own distinctive shape,
Dark silhouettes across the white sky,
Wide, strong trunks and branches
Tapering upward to delicate clusters.
We don't notice trees. When the leaves
Cover them or the bright snow distracts
Our gaze, we just don't see them;
They fade into the background.

Take a good look at them now.

FOREST PRIMEVAL

I like old things that people ignore,
Like clusters of trees near the highway.
In a car, you rarely notice them,
These survivors of cutting and bulldozing
And paving. They're at the edges of roads,
Sometimes in the middle of roads.
Some have been set aside on purpose,
To counteract the asphalt.
Some are simply odd patches, too small
Or uneven to build something on
(Even a Dunkin Donuts).
These are places no one goes to,
And few people even look at.
With the cars zipping by, it's too dangerous
For most animals to get to them. Only birds
Make use of them - you can spot a solitary hawk
Perched on a branch, or watch a flock of crows
Squawking in the trees. And in the bushes
You can hear songbirds, chirping away
In the midst of the traffic.
Most of the trees are pines, some of them
Quite ancient, some new-grown.
Walking among them, you can feel
A thick cushion of ancient foliage
Beneath your feet. You could be walking
In a forest from colonial times,
And, in fact, you are.

OLD NEIGHBORHOOD

It looks almost the same.
There's the curb, then a three-foot strip of grass,
Then a slab of concrete sidewalk,
Then the neatly trimmed lawns, then
The houses. The houses are close together,
With only two-lane, concrete driveways
Between them. They're in a row,
All of them the same, short distance
From the sidewalk -about fifteen feet.
All the houses have two stories, and
Most of them have front porches
To sit on in the summer. They're similar,
But not the same. Each house has
Some special touch to make it different.

It's 2017 and I'm in Saratoga Springs,
New York. But it could be 1947 in Framingham,
Mass., and I could be walking down
Henry Street, the street where I grew up.
I guess they set up neighborhoods
The same way back in the day: the same row
Of two-story houses, close together
And close to the road; the same driveways,
The same sidewalks, the same front lawns.
There were the Bradleys across from us,
The Camerons on the right, and the Frosts
On our left. I was afraid of Mrs. Frost.
If I put one foot on her precious lawn,
She'd pull back the lace curtain and rap
On the window. Her husband, though, was my friend.
He had a serious collection of exotic insects,
And he liked to show it to the little boy next door.
Mrs. Cameron bought seeds from me every spring,

(Though I never saw her plant a garden).
Mrs. Bradley let us kids play in her back yard
With her fluffy white dog. On Henry Street,
All the old cliches actually happened:
Waverly Farm delivered milk with cream
On the top, and, one summer, an organ grinder
Came by in a big, open truck.

Walking down this street in Saratoga,
I can feel it all coming back.

POLAND

We're at 7:30 mass in a salt mine deep under the earth.
The Poles have been mining salt here since 1280.
We're in a huge, high-ceilinged chamber. Everything here
Has been carved from salt - the ceiling, the walls, the floor,
The bas-reliefs on the walls, the statue of John Paul II.
The audience has come down in seven-person elevators.
Most are Poles. Only a few are visitors, like my wife and me.
A bells sounds. Seven men in clerical garb stride
From the back to the altar - the celebrant in priestly robes,
The attendants in simpler gowns. They play
The traditional roles. The elderly celebrant reads
The opening prayers; A young acolyte reads the gospel;
A tall, austere Franciscan gives the sermon.

But the laity participate, too.
A middle-aged woman comes up from the audience
To read the epistle - she's wearing blue jeans
And sneakers (Nikes). A second woman,
Slightly younger, also in jeans and sneakers
(Polish made?), comes up to lead the singing.
At communion, there are no benches and we all
Kneel directly on the hard salt floor. As I kneel there,
I watch the crowd move forward to the altar.
There are as many young people as older ones
(Unlike in America). Two older men are wearing suits
And dress shoes, but the rest are dressed
For an ordinary day. Most of them - old and young,
Women and men - are wearing sneakers.

71

PAST AND PRESENT

SUNDAY MORNING

Lots of white heads in this church,
A full three-quarters of the people.
Most of the others are children -
Grandchildren, most likely.
Where are their parents, the middle
Generation, the working adults?
How long can a church of old folks
And children survive?

It's not as hopeless as it seems.
The church, after all, is almost full,
And the people are paying attention.
They even sing the hymns.
Perhaps the middle- agers are taking
A little break, just as most of us do,
Just as I did. My little break lasted
Twenty years or so.

But I'm back here now.
And so are all the other old folks,
And many of the middle generation
Will find their way back, too.
This church of old folks and children
Is already two thousand years old.
It's solid. It's not going to crumble
Any time soon.

Summer Day

This is a perfect summer afternoon,
Warm, but not hot or humid,
With a light breeze moving the air.
Nothing else seems to be moving.
Time itself seems to have stopped.

I sit in the sun, my eyes closed, feeling
The light glow through my eyelids,
Taking in the sounds of the season:
The faint shouts from the bathing beach,
The chattering of the birds.

For a moment, there's no traffic,
(The tourists are all at the beach.)
And the village feels like it used to look,
With ladies in hats and long dresses
Strolling beside an unpaved road.

El Pancho Grande

This all started with a look in the mirror.
I didn't like what I saw there. It reminded me
Of "El Rancho Grande," A Mexican cowboy song
My sixth grade class sang in the Jr. High musical.
We boys in the back changed the words
To "El Pancho Grande." It was a big joke then,
But now the pancho grande is on me.

I've remembered that old song all these years.
I can still sing it - in Spanish, no less -
But I've never known what the words mean.
Translations I've found still leave me puzzled:
On the big ranch, a merry ranch-girl
Wants to make this guy some rancher's pants.
She'll start with wool and end with leather.

O.K., sounds like a way to make rancher's pants,
But what the hell is really going on? Who is this guy,
And why does he need new pants? Has he worn
Through his old ones? Are his cojones hanging out
(You can guess that one)? Why does the little ranch-girl
Care about his pants? And why is she so merry?
Did Miss Anderson check this song out?

Ah, for the days of innocent jokes,
And panchos not yet grande.

ADAM AGAIN

(*A Scene from the movie "Youth"*)

You're an eighty-year-old guy,
Immersed in a swimming pool up to your neck,
When a beautiful woman, completely naked,
Walks to the water in front of you.
She looks at you briefly with an even gaze
And moves, unhurried, to the other side
Of the pool, where she now reclines, her body
Beneath the water and only her head exposed.

This woman's body is perfect, flawless -
Eve herself couldn't have been more perfect
At her creation- and you're an old guy
With a bulging belly and white hairless legs.
But, looking at her, you're Adam again,
Amazed at this wondrous gift.

HOVERING

When I was younger, I used to be good
With older people. When they talked,
I didn't jump in with my own thoughts.
I'd ask an occasional question and listen.
I learned a lot of things from them:
What it was like to fix the phone lines
After an ice storm; why there's
A long hollow beside Chelsea Road
(A train line used to run there);
What a threat appendicitis used to be.

If we were walking, I'd kind of hover
At an old person's side, ready
To grab an elbow if the need arose.
And the need did arise. I recall
Pulling Uncle Maurice from the path
Of a city bus, or catching my mother
Before she toppled off the cliff walk.
That last save was pretty obvious,
But, usually, I leant a hand so gently
That my companion barely noticed.

Lately, I myself have noticed
That certain younger people tend
To hover at my side while we're walking.
I don't call them on it, but I know
What they're up to.

WINTER

OLD MAINERS

What y'r seein' ain't the real Maine, y'know.
You come up here in summer lookin' for it,
But that's the time it's hard to find.
For us, summer's just the stretch
From one winter to another.
Maine's a winter state, and we
Don't fit Into your summer scenes.

You have to look real close
Just to find us. Like that fella there
With the long white beard. Or that fella
In that red and black wool shirt,
Sittin' there sweatin' (and scratchin').
Or that ol' man in the extra-tight pants
(Still wearin' his longjohns, dont'cha know).

They look out of place in all this heat,
Like those damn fools wearin'
Sawed-off pants in the snow.
In winter, though, they look comfortable,
Like they're where they belong.

THE MIDDLE OF APRIL

This year, mid-April
Is neither winter nor spring.
The snow is gone, but there's no trace
Of green on the bushes or trees.
Last fall's dead leaves have reappeared
And cover the forest floor.
The woods look like a cemetery
No one cares for: dead trees
And limbs litter the ground,
Or hang and lean at random angles.

I hate to see winter end,
And on a cold, bleak day like this,
I can almost convince myself
That winter is still with us.
But I know it's not. This winter's gone,
And it wasn't that much to begin with.
I miss the winters we had back in the day,
Real, old-time winters, when the drifts
Lasted into May, and you could still ski
In the middle of April.

FLORIDA

Even in New England,
Where winter is so glorious,
People assume you hate it.
"Well, at least it didn't snow,"
They chortle, after a batch of rain
And sleet has set winter back
Another week. They tell you
Their Florida plans with such joy
That you have to feel happy for them,
Even if Florida is the last place on earth
You'd ever go in winter.

Myself, I've always loved winter.
I'm an old guy now, but,
When I see the first snow falling,
I'm just like those kids on T.V.
Who jump up and down,
Shouting "Snow, snow!"
And when the morning sun hits
The fresh snow clustered in the pine trees,
Who could even think of leaving?

OLD SKIER

It was a cold morning -
Just about zero- and the snow
Squeaked a little as we skied.
Still, we got a decent glide
And were moving right along.

Skiing towards us was an old man,
Moving very slowly. He'd been out
A while - his mustache, hair,
And eyebrows were heavy with frost.
He might have noticed us
Passing by, but he didn't return
Our greeting. His eyes were closed
And he was singing, very softly,
To himself.

He disappeared around a corner,
Leaving us all wondering. Who was he?
Where did he come from?
He could have been Old Man Winter.
Maybe he was.

Epilogue

FIRST TO GO

I guess I've just assumed,
Because I'm eleven years older,
That I'd be the first to go,
But our family histories suggest
I could be wrong.
If she went first, she'd be spared
The pain of grieving -
At least I'd be glad about that.
But how would I get along?
Who would I talk to?
Who would I do things with?
Who would drive me to the gym
At six in the morning?
Who would make me take my pills
And use the damn seat belt?

If you're an old guy
And your wife dies, what do you
Do then? There's no Plan B.
Hell, there's no Plan A.

Printed in the USA
CPSIA information can be obtained
at www.ICGtesting.com
CBHW031513090724
11329CB00008B/290